# Contents

## *Illustrations*

## *Abstract*

Our reliance on computers and information-based technologies within DOD has greatly increased our potential for vulnerability if our information systems are attacked. DOD systems now receive numerous intrusion attempts daily and this trend appears to be increasing. It is paramount that DOD develops appropriate defensive courses of action to systematically and appropriately counter the threat of future cyber attacks. The main problem is distinguishing the type of intrusion or attack and developing the mechanisms to appropriately respond whether by law enforcement or military action. This paper develops a spectrum of cyber conflict from hacking to information warfare which addresses who the adversary is, their intentions and how best to counter them.

This spectrum of cyber conflict will consist of various forms of cyber attack such as hacking, hacktivism (a form of computer based civil disobedience), espionage, terrorism, and information warfare. The important issue in countering any form of cyber attack is to quickly discern the type of attack and adversary and respond appropriately. Currently, tracking down computer intrusions is a law enforcement function. The collection of information/evidence after the fact to trace the attacks back to the origin requires a robust and competent law enforcement community. The traditional war fighting military is prohibited from executing this mission domestically. If the US is a law enforcement theatre, now domestic law enforcement has a critical role in national security and national defense. This paper will develop a spectrum of cyber-conflict and answer the question of when law enforcement or the military should respond to cyber attacks against US and DOD critical information systems.

# Chapter 1

# Introduction

*The form of any war—and it is the form which is of primary interest to men of war—depends on the technical means of war available.*

Giulio Douhet

The United States must be able to deter computer attacks against our critical information infrastructure. A strong deterrence policy involves both a strong defense and the threat of retaliation or punishment. Despite a strong defense to deny cyber attackers access to our systems, we remain vulnerable because it is nearly impossible to stop all intrusions. Therefore, we must be able to punish or retaliate against individuals, sub-state groups or states that are responsible for cyber attacks. This ability to retaliate involves more than just an offensive information warfare capability. In most cases, the DOD must use US law enforcement to assist in identifying and locating the perpetrator. In the realm of cyber defense, law enforcement now plays a critical role in national security and national defense.

Our reliance on computers and information-based technologies within DOD has greatly increased the vulnerability of our military forces if our information systems are attacked. DOD systems now receive numerous intrusion attempts daily and this trend appears to be increasing. In 1994 the total of network attacks reported throughout DOD was only 225. By 1999, the total number of reported events was just over 22,000, and if the trend continues, there will be over 24,000 by year's end.[1] This increased threat of network attack has highlighted a new US vulnerability and increased the importance of defensive information warfare for the US military.

There is much written on the subject of information warfare and how this new type of warfare will affect and shape the future of war. The discussion of information warfare always deals with both offensive and defensive information operations and discusses our ability to defend and deter against information warfare attack. It is logical to categorize defending against cyber warfare in traditional military terms when military terms are used to explain and define this concept called information warfare. Unfortunately, this broad generalization of information warfare and defense against information attack neglects one fundamental difference between traditional warfare and information warfare. The difference is that an attack against our information infrastructures located in the United States is actually a crime and must be countered within the legal requirements and jurisdictions of US code.

The very nature of defending our critical national infrastructure from an information warfare attack cannot be viewed in a traditional military sense and must be thought of and countered differently than traditional warfare. A strong defense against information warfare attack can be effective either by denial or a threat of punishment. Denial against information attack rests on very strong defenses so that an aggressor cannot achieve his objective and requires effective identification and authentication mechanisms. The threat of punishment or governmental reprisal against an attacker requires identifiable targets that can be located and attacked and relies on auditing and trace-back methods.[2]

The US military has focused a large proportion of its efforts on denying and preventing cyber attacks and rightly so. It is paramount that we do everything within our power to deny the adversary access or the ability to attack our systems. Unfortunately, we can never be 100 percent certain that our systems are invulnerable to attack. Cyber attackers can always find trapdoors and glitches in software that allow them to get around obstacles; or, if that fails, they can try launching very sophisticated password cracking programs. This vulnerability was highlighted after a 1998 investigation at a Department of Energy Laboratory, where a hack had shut down the facility for a few weeks. After this event, systems security administrators were running a password-cracking program to help assess and limit the risk of future intrusion. But, even after a year, their program was still able to guess one in ten new passwords every week.[3] Based on this inherent fallibility with information systems, especially as network linkage increases, we can never totally rely on a strategy of denial. Therefore, it is important to also address deterrence and the ability to counter cyber attack by threat of punishment or military reprisal.

The important issue in countering a cyber-attack through threat of reprisal is to discern the type of attack, identify the adversary and respond appropriately. Given the current US national information infrastructure (NII) and the US military's reliance on the NII, most cases of identifying the perpetrator of an information warfare attack or any attack against DOD systems will be the responsibility of US law enforcement. In most cases, the traditional war fighting military is prohibited from executing this mission domestically because of US laws.

This paper will discuss this critical role for law enforcement in national security and national defense. Part I of this paper will detail categories or types of computer attacks and will look at the intentions of the perpetrator. The type of computer attack and intentions will be categorized into levels of conflict ranging from illegal computer hacking, hacktivism, computer espionage, computer terrorism and information warfare. Part II will further explore the technical and legal difficulties in determining the identity and location of the perpetrator. Part III will discuss the spectrum of cyber conflict which will be a synthesis of the type of computer attack, identity, location and intention of the perpetrator and the appropriate response by either law enforcement or the military to counter each broad category of attack.

This spectrum of cyber-conflict will show the correlation between computer attacks and criminal activity and highlight why the US military cannot counter or respond to information attacks until after the perpetrator is identified. DOD must develop a robust law enforcement function to assist in a strategy of countering cyber attacks. Without law enforcement's assistance, appropriate US government reprisals such as criminal punishment or US national policy responses in the form of diplomatic or economic sanctions or military reprisals will not be possible. Finally, without this credible response capability, the US will lack the vital ability to deter future network attacks.

**Notes**

[1] Robert C. West, "The cyber-defence force's virtual shield," *Janes Intelligence Review*, 01 December 2000, n.p; on-line, 2000 Jane's Information Group, 28 December 2000.
[2] Roger W. Barnett, "Information Operations, Deterrence, and the Use of Force"; *Naval War College Review*, Spring 1998, n.p.; on-line, Internet, 13 November 2000, available from http://www.nwc.navy.mil/press/review/1998/spring.
[3] John Arquilla, "Screen Saver", *New Republic*, 01 May 2000, Vol. 222 Issue 18, p16, 3p, 1c, on-line, Academic Search Elite, 25 October 2000.

# Chapter 2

# Types of Computer Attacks

## Intentional or Unintentional Actors

This study will divide the types of computer attacks into two distinct categories based on the intent of the perpetrator of the computer intrusion. This differentiation can be defined as intentional cyber warfare attack (IA) with intentional actors (I-actors) or Unintentional cyber warfare attack (UA) with U-actors (unintentional cyber actors).[1] An intentional cyber warfare attack (IA) is any attack through cyber-means to intentionally affect national security (cyber warfare) or to further operations against national security. IA can be equated to warfare; it is national policy at the level of warfare. It includes any act intended to compel an opponent to fulfill national will, executed against an opponent's computer and software systems.[2]

"Unintentional cyber actors are individuals who unintentionally attack but affect national security and are largely unaware of the international ramifications of their actions. U-actors include anyone who commits cyber infiltration and penetrates the defenses of a system such that the system can be manipulated, assaulted, or raided."[3] U-actors have a large variety of motivations and intentions but do not intend on inflicting damage to national security or to further operations against national security. These U-actors can be categorized as hackers and although they commit cyber crime, they are not intentionally prosecuting cyber warfare. It is important to note that unintentional actors may be influenced by I-actors but are unaware they are being manipulated to participate in cyber operations. [4]

## Cyber Crime (Illegal Exploration and Hacking)

The first type of computer attack combines several different types of unintentional actors into one category defined as cyber crime or "hacker". Although this category of hacker includes many kinds of cyber criminals, from a DOD perspective, the motivation of a hacker without intent to damage the national security of the United States is the importance difference. Therefore, it is necessary to differentiate between cyber crime and other levels of computer attack because it will affect the type of DOD response.

Cyber crime in the form of a cyber intrusion (hacking) is illegal access into a network system and can range from simple exploration causing no damage to malicious hackers who are intent on causing loss or damage.[5] Most information systems tend to divide the world into at least three parts: outsiders, users, and superusers. A popular route of attack for hackers is first to use a password attack so that the outsider becomes a user, and then once a user, he will use known weaknesses of Unix programs so that he can access superuser privileges. Once a superuser, a hacker can read or alter files; control the system; make it easier to re-enter the system (even after tougher security measures are enforced); and insert rogue code (e.g., a virus, logic bomb, Trojan Horse, etc.[6]) for later exploitation.[7] Although the other levels of cyber-attack to include cyber-espionage, cyber-terrorism and information warfare also use a similar method of hacking into an internet connected system, the main distinction between a hacker and the other levels is the intention of the perpetrator.

In his book, "Fighting Computer Crime", Wiley identifies several types of cyber criminals. They range from pranksters who perpetrate tricks on others to career criminals. Pranksters generally do not intend any particular or long-lasting harm. Wiley identifies hackers as individuals who explore other's computer systems for education, out of curiosity, to achieve idealized social justice or to compete with their peers. They may be attempting to gain the use of a more powerful computer, gain respect from fellow hackers, build a reputation, or gain acceptance as an expert without formal education. Malicious Hackers, sometimes called crackers, are intent on causing loss (in contrast to achieving illegal gain) to satisfy some antisocial motives. Many computer virus creators and distributors also fall into this category.

Another form of cyber criminal is the career criminal. These individuals earn part or all of their income from crime, although they do not necessarily engage in crime as a full time occupation. Some have a job and steal a little and then move on to another job to repeat the process. In some cases they conspire with others or work within organized crime gangs such as the Mafia. According to the FBI, many of these criminal alliances use advanced information technology and encrypted communications to elude capture.[8]

In most cases, hackers who are intent on penetrating DOD systems are doing it for the challenge and thrill. Hackers are motivated by a variety of factors, including thrill, challenge, pleasure, knowledge, recognition, power and friendship.[9]

> In a survey of 164 hackers, the three main reasons for hacking were (in decreasing order) challenge, knowledge, and pleasure, all of which are positive aspects beneficial to discovery learning. These accounted for nearly half (49%) of the reasons cited. Another 24% were attributed to recognition, excitement, (of doing something illegal), and friendship. The remaining 27% were ascribed to self-gratification, addiction, espionage, theft, profit, vengeance, sabotage, and freedom.[10]

The Centre for Infrastructural Warfare Studies estimated in December 1997 that there were fewer than 1,000 professional hackers worldwide at the time. They defined 'professional hacker' as someone who is 'capable of building and creating original cracking methods'. He has superior programming skills in a number of machine languages and has original knowledge of telecommunications networks. In terms of objectives, his goals are usually financial[11]

This first group of cyber criminals or "hackers" can be categorized as Unintentional Cyber actors. Although they have a variety of motivations ranging from simple exploration to criminal intent to defraud or financially gain in some manner, they are not considered intentional cyber actors targeting national security. Because they are simply criminals, a DOD response to these types of cyber attacks should be considered as a legal response to stop and prosecute criminal actors.

## Hacktivism

A new phenomenon in the spectrum of cyber conflict has emerged and can be described as electronic disobedience or hacktivism. Computerized activism operates in the tradition of non-violent direct action and civil disobedience and borrows the tactics of trespass and blockade from earlier social movements and applies them to the Internet.[12]

> A typical civil disobedience tactic is a 'sit-in' in which groups of people physically blockade, with their bodies, the entranceways of an opponent's office or physically occupy an opponent's office. Electronic Civil Disobedience, as a form of mass decentered electronic direct action, utilizes virtual blockades and virtual sit-ins. Unlike the participant in a traditional civil disobedience action, an ECD actor can participate in virtual blockades and sit-ins from home, from work, from the university, or from other points of access to the Net.[13]

The origins of computerized activism extend back in pre-Web history to the mid-1980s. However, Hacktivism remained marginal to political and social movements until the explosion of the Internet in the mid-1990s. Now, in the post-Web Internet phase, there is widespread use by a large number of grassroots groups and other political actors in countries all over the world. There have been reports of hacktivity in Britain, Australia, India, China, and on almost every continent. [14]

In the spring of 1998, a young British hacker known as "JF" accessed about 300 web sites. He replaced the sites' homepages with an image of a mushroom cloud and an 800-word declaration that began "This mass takeover goes out to all the people out there who want to see peace in this world". Some affected sites were Web servers at India's atomic research center and the Saudi Royal Family. [15] At that point, it was the biggest political hack of its kind. Since then, there have been numerous reports of web sites being accessed and altered with political content. [16]

The desired goal of Hacktivism is to draw attention to particular issues by engaging in actions that are unusual and will attract some degree of media coverage. While it may be too early to make accurate predictions, the threat of Hacktivism has yet to be fully recognized or tested. It is important to include this new threat against DOD systems and understand the possible long term consequences posed for governments and states if groups of individual protestors can engage in forms of cyber space resistance across traditional geo-political borders. [17]

Hacktivism is distinct from hacking in the purely criminal sense because it represents a political motivation with intent to not only do harm to a system, but to influence the public and government that it is protesting with its electronic civil disobedience. In some cases, if a large enough group of protesters from around the globe can launch an electronic attack, it has the potential to cause major damage and may be difficult to differentiate from an initial information warfare attack. Although, Hacktivism is also a criminal act, it is distinct because of the perpetrator's political intentions and may require a different if not unique response from the DOD or US government.

## Computer Espionage

The next level of threat to the DOD and US national security is cyber espionage. This threat is likely to be the most difficult to distinguish because it may appear to be hacker activity and will intentionally avoid causing damage or harm in order to avoid detection. Although there is little information in the public domain about the use of computer hacking in foreign intelligence operations, there is no doubt that this activity is prevalent among most state intelligence agencies around the world. The first documented computer espionage case was in 1986 and was immortalized in the best seller novel, "The Cuckoos Egg". In this case, the Soviet KGB levied five hackers (to include the Hanover Hacker) to hack into US DOD systems and provide information to the Soviets. These young hackers all had drug and financial problems and were easily exploited by the Soviet KGB.[18] This early espionage investigation revealed the importance of cyber espionage to foreign intelligence services and also the proclivity for criminal hackers to be vetted and employed by foreign intelligence services.

> According to Peter Schweizer's book *Friendly Spies,* Germany initiated one such (intelligence) program, dubbed Project Rehab after the harlot who helped the Israelites infiltrate Jericho, in the mid-1980s. The project was developed within Germany's intelligence agency, the Bundes Nacrichten Dienst (BND), as a joint effort between the BND's central office and the divisions for human and signals intelligence. The unit allegedly accessed computer systems in the United States, the former

Soviet Union, Japan, France, Italy, and Great Britain, and in 1991 penetrated the Society for Worldwide Interbank Financial Telecommunications (SWIFT) network, which carries most international bank transfers.[19]

These popular books "The Cuckoo's Nest" and "Friendly Spies" highlights the potential threat of foreign intelligence cyber operations against US and DOD information systems.

## Computer Terrorism

The next threat identified on the spectrum of cyber attack is cyber terrorism. Barry Collin, a senior research fellow at the Institute for Security and Intelligence in California, established the term "cyber terrorism" to refer to the convergence of cyber space and terrorism.[20] Mark Pollitt, special agent for the FBI, offers a working definition: "Cyber terrorism is the premeditated, politically motivated attack against information, computer systems, computer programs, and data which result in violence against noncombatant targets by subnational groups or clandestine agents."[21]

Early indications suggest that terrorist groups may use the Internet more to influence public perception and coordinate their activities than to launch highly destructive and disruptive attacks.[22] An example can be found in the struggle between Zapatista National Liberation Army (EZLN) and the government of Mexico. The Zapatistas and their supporters have used the Internet to spread word about their situation and to coordinate activities. One group of New York supporters, the Electronic Disturbance Theater (EDT) organized an attack against Mexican President Zedillo's Web site. On April 10, 1998, participants in the attack pointed their web browsers to a site with FloodNet software, which bombarded the site with traffic.[23]

On September 9, 1998, EDT once again struck the Web site of President Zedillo, along with those of the Pentagon and the Frankfurt Stock exchange. The Net strike was launched in conjunction with the Arts Electronic Festival in Infowar, held in Liz, Austria. According to Brett Stalbaum, author of the FloodNet software used in the attack, the Pentagon was chosen because "we believe that the US military trained the soldiers carrying out the human rights abuses." Stalbaum said the Frankfurt Stock Exchange was chosen because is represented globalization, which was at the root of the Chiapas' problems. EDT estimated that up to 10,000 people participated in the demonstration delivering 600,000 hits per minute to each of the three sites. The Web servers operated by the Pentagon and the Mexican government struck back. When they sensed an attack from the FloodNet servers, they launched a counter-offensive against the users' browsers, in some cases forcing the protestors to reboot their computers. The Frankfurt stock Exchange reported that they normally get 6 million hits a day and that services appeared unaffected."[24]

Although this may be more of an example of hacktivism on the part of the EDT, it shows how a terrorist organization can use the Internet to broadcast their message and misdirect or misinform the general population in multiple nations simultaneously.[25]

Another form of cyber terrorism is known as "cybotage" which includes acts of disruption and destruction against information infrastructures by terrorists who learn the skills of cyber attack. Although most experts still believe that terrorism will continue to focus on lethal, destructive acts, there is also the belief that some terrorist will stress disruption over destruction. These networked terrorists will no doubt continue to destroy things and kill people, but their principal strategy may move toward the nonlethal end of the spectrum, where command and control nodes and vulnerable information infrastructures provide rich sets of targets.[26]

Whether cyber terrorism in the future is used more as a means to influence public perception or as a forum to conduct politically motivated network attacks, most experts agree that terrorist groups will increase their use of computers to intimidate and coerce societies and governments.

Before the US Senate Judiciary Committee, Clark Staten, executive director of the Emergency Response and Research Institute (ERRI) in Chicago, testified that it was believed that 'members of some Islamic extremist organizations have been attempting to develop a 'hacker network' to support their computer activities and even engage in offensive information warfare attacks in the future.[27]

The increased threat of cyber terrorism by sub state or state sponsored actors against the US national infrastructure will require the US to identify and retaliate against cyber terrorist attacks in order to deter and prevent future attacks.

## Cyber Warfare

The highest level of threat on the spectrum of cyber conflict is cyber warfare. Defining exactly what is meant by cyber or information warfare can be difficult and encompasses many aspects of traditional attacks against information systems and also warfare waged by using computer systems to attack computer network or software systems. For the purpose of this paper, cyber warfare will be defined as the "use of computer intrusion techniques and other capabilities against an adversary's information-based infrastructure"[28] to intentionally affect national security or to further operations against national security[29]. The basic tools for attack such as the computer, modem, telephone, and software, are essentially the same as those used by other actors on the spectrum of cyber conflict.

If the basic cyber attack tools and skills are common across the spectrum, it may be difficult to distinguish recreational hackers from Information Warriors. Said another way:

An IW attack against US infrastructures may be little more than a series of hacker attacks, conducted against carefully chosen targets, synchronized in time, to accomplish specific purposes. An adversary could combine cyber attacks with physical attacks in an effort to paralyze or panic large segments of society. It could damage our capability to respond to incidents (by disabling the 911 system or emergency communications, for example), hamper our ability to deploy conventional military forces, and otherwise limit the freedom of action of our national leadership.[30]

In most cases, the only way to differentiate between a hacker or cyber warfare attack may be in the intensity, organization or damage of the attack and perhaps only if it is conducted in conjunction with other traditional warfare attacks or a declaration of war by an enemy state.

This difficulty in distinguishing between the type of attack on the cyber conflict spectrum exposes the most important issue in defining the type of cyber threat. The definition must include identity of the perpetrator and his intentions. During an attack, we may not know if it is cyber war unless it is in conjunction with a traditional war against a known enemy. It could also be an act of cyber crime, hacktivism, or cyber terrorism. The key issue will be who is the perpetrator and what are his intentions. .

**Notes**

[1] (see appendix A) Lt Col Lionel D. Alford, Jr., USAF, "Cyber Warfare: Protecting Military Systems", *The Journal of the Defense Acquisition University Review Quarterly* 7, no. 2., (Spring 2000): 105.

[2] Ibid.

[3] Ibid.

[4] Ibid.

[5] Donn B. Parker, *Fighting Computer Crime,* (New York: Wiley Computer Publishing, 1998), 144-145.

[6] A virus is a fragment of code that attaches itself to other computer instructions including software application code, the code used to boot a computer or macro instructions place in documents. When activated a virus may then execute a "payload" which can do anything from displaying an amusing message to wiping out files on the hard drive. A logic bomb is a program with malicious code that lies dormant until some event occurs, at which point it executes. If a date or time triggers execution, as is often the case, the program is also called a "time bomb". A software Trojan Horse is a program that, when activated, performs some undesirable action not anticipated by the person running it. It could delete files, reformat a disk, or leak sensitive data back to its author. This malicious program is typically hidden inside a systems or application program that looks innocent. The Trojan version might be distributed through email or posted on the Web.

**Notes**

[7] Martin C. Libicki, "Protecting the United States in Cyberspace," in *Cyberwar: Security, Strategy, and Conflict in the Information Age,* ed. Alan D. Capen, Douglas H. Dearth and R. Thomas Gooden, (Fairfax, Virgina: AFCEA International Press, May 1996), 92.

[8] Parker, 144-145.

[9] Dorothy E. Denning, *Information Warfare and Security* (Reading, MA: Addison Wesley Longman, Inc, 1998), 45.

[10] Ibid., 47.

[11] Ibid., 51.

[12] Stephan Wray, "Electronic Civil Disobedience and the World Wide Web of Hacktivism: A Mapping of Extraparliamentarian Direct Action Net Politics," *A paper for The world Wide Web and Contemporary Cultural Theory Conference,* (Drake University: November 1998) n.p.; on-line, Internet, 17 January 2001, available from http: //www.nyu.edu/ projects/wray/ ecd.html.

[13] Ibid.

[14] Ibid.

[15] James Glave, "Anti-Nuke Cracker Strikes Again," for Wired News, 3 July 98, n.p., on-line, Internet, available from http://www.thing.net/~rdom/ecd/Brithacker.html, 2 March 01.

[16] Ibid.

[17] Ibid.

[18] Jim Christy, Supervisory Special Agent, Defense Wide Information Assurance Program, Assistant Secretary of Defense Command Control Communications and Intelligence (ASDC3I/DIAP), Pentagon interviewed by author, 14 November 2000.

[19] Denning, 64.

[20] Ibid., 69.

[21] Ibid.

[22] Ibid., 71.

[23] Ibid., 68.

[24] Ibid., 74.

[25] Ibid., 68.

[26] John Arquilla, David Ronfeldt, and Michele Zanini, "Information Age Terrorism," in *Countering the New Terrorism*, ed. Ian O. Lesser et al. RAND Report MR-989-AF (Santa Monica, California: RAND, 1998), 71.

[27] Denning, 68.

[28] West, 17-18.

[29] Alford, 105.

[30] Ibid.

# Chapter 3

# Determination of Perpetrator

If the Department of Defense wants to have the ability to retaliate against a computer attack whether it is a cyber crime or a cyber warfare attack, they must be able to determine who has committed the attack and their intentions. This chapter will explore the technical and legal difficulties with determining who the perpetrator is and address the necessity for DOD to establish a strong operational relationship with both civil and military law enforcement organizations in order to be able to react quickly to potential cyber warfare.

## Technical Limitations

The vast array of public and private networks connecting computers and users all over the globe is known as cyberspace. Indeed, it is often characterized as a "virtual world" that transcends space. People log onto computers and on-line services without regard to their own geographic location or the location of the system they enter. Computers are addressed through domain names such as "abc.xyz.com," which give no indication of physical location. Similarly, individuals correspond using domain-based addresses such as "smith@abc.xyz.com". [1]

> Because a user may be able to log into a computer from anyplace in the world (e.g., using telnet or a dial-up line), there is no way of identifying the geographic location of a user even when the location of the computer

where the account is held is known. With mobile phones and computing, the location of the user becomes even more difficult to determine. The consequence of this lack of grounding in physical space is that actions can take place in cyberspace without anyone knowing exactly where they originated and the jurisdictions effected. [2]

Finding the perpetrator of a computer intrusion or any crime in cyberspace is extremely difficult and often impossible, especially when the perpetrator has "looped" through numerous machines throughout the world to get to a target. [3] Figure 1 shows an example of how a hacker in New York City may weave and loop through a government computer in Latvia, to a computer belonging to the NY times, through GW University in Washington DC and finally to his final target, an Air Force system in Tampa, Florida.

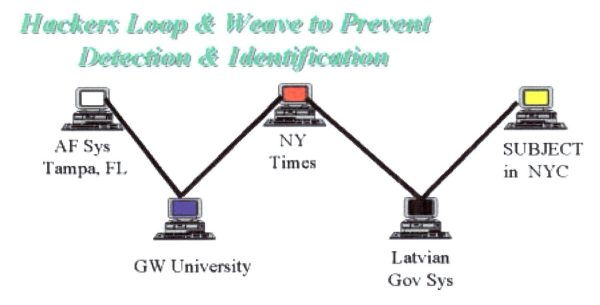

**Figure 1 Hackers Loop & Weave to Prevent Detection and Identification[4]**

This technical difficulty in locating and identifying the perpetrator can be overcome by several law enforcement methods. These methods consist of packet sniffers, keystroke monitoring, and other environmental surveillance methods such as cameras, imagery systems and electromagnetic signal reception. Designed and developed by the FBI, the most common law enforcement diagnostic tool is a packet sniffer, which has recently become well known by the name "Carnivore." A sniffer such as "Carnivore" placed on any computer connected to the network can read all messages flowing through the network regardless of their destination. Whereas a machine would normally be configured to read only messages that are addressed to it, it can be set to "promiscuous mode" so that it sees all traffic. In addition, it can also be configured to ignore those communications which they (FBI) are not authorized to intercept.[5]

The Carnivore device provides the FBI with a "surgical" ability to intercept and collect the communications, which are the subject of the lawful order. This type of tool is necessary to meet the stringent requirements of the federal wiretapping statutes. The Carnivore device works much like commercial "sniffers" and other network diagnostic tools used by Internet Service Providers (ISPs) every day, except that it provides the FBI with a unique ability to distinguish between communications which may be lawfully intercepted and those which may not. For example, if a court order provides for the lawful interception of one type of communication (e.g., e-mail), but excludes all other communications (e.g., online shopping), the Carnivore tool can be configured to intercept only those e-mails being transmitted either to or from the named subject. Carnivore serves to limit the messages viewable by human eyes to those, which are strictly included within the court order. ISP knowledge and assistance, as directed by court order, is required to install the device.[6]

In 1995, federal agents, using a packet sniffer, traced down an Argentine student who had hacked into a system at Harvard University.

> The hacker was using the Harvard network as a springboard to hack into Defense Department systems including the Naval Research Laboratory and Los Alamos National Laboratory. After a court order was issued, investigators placed a computer between Harvard's network and the

Internet and set it to scan for messages that appeared to come from the hacker. By sifting through the messages, they traced the attacks to Julio Cesar Ardita, a 21-year-old university student located in Argentina. During this process, four separate screening procedures were used to protect the privacy of other users on the network. Ardita eventually pled guilty to illegal wiretapping and computer crime felonies and was sentenced to 3 years probation and a $5,000 fine.[7]

Federal investigators have the technology to track down a hacker both inside and outside the United States; however, it still involves many legal barriers to include court-ordered wiretaps, which can take weeks to obtain.

## Legal Limitations

Law enforcement agencies face many challenges in responding to information attacks in cyber space, particularly attacks that cross national and regional borders and exploit technologies of concealment. It can be difficult to locate a hacker who has looped through multiple systems, used anonymous services, or entered through a wireless connection from a mobile unit. Another challenge is collection and preservation of evidence. Evidence may be encrypted or dispersed across several countries. Tracking an intruder who has used a computer located in the United States will require searches and seizures or wiretaps. These searches may encompass multiple jurisdictions and many laws are not uniform across jurisdictions. Also, many countries have weak laws or no laws at all, against some computer hacking activity. Even if laws exist, extradition may be prohibited, depending on agreements between countries.[8]

Figure 2 highlights the jurisdictional problems with tracking a hacker who has used several computer systems to illegally gain access to AF Systems in Tampa, FL. Each location requires a separate court order from a court with jurisdiction for the geographic location of the computer system that is used. Although, law enforcement agencies have the technology to trace back to the origin of the hacker, each time they access another computer system in the United States, they must have legal authorization to do so. This can cause many delays and difficulties in obtaining the evidence and identifying and eventually locating the perpetrator of a computer attack. [9]

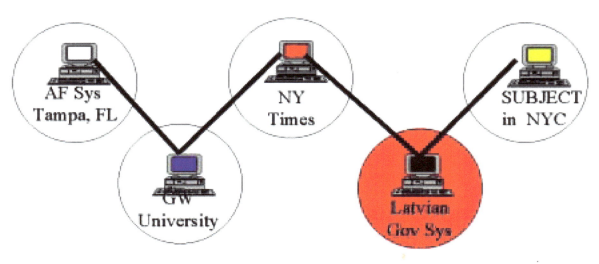

**Figure 2 Court Jurisdiction based on Geography**[10]

It is this area of identifying the perpetrator of a computer attack that causes the most difficulty for the Department of Defense. The first line of defense is to prevent the attack or intrusion from occurring. However, a strong defense from attack will never be able to completely eliminate all attacks. When an attack occurs, there will be many times when it will be vital for DOD to determine the identity of the intruder and their intentions, whether they be an intentional actor with intent to affect national security or not. It will be impossible for DOD to respond to these actors or for the United States government to take other actions such as economic sanctions or military action without definitely knowing the identity of the perpetrator. As long as the perpetrator uses computer systems located within the United States, DOD will be restricted by law from tracing these actors without assistance from law enforcement agencies using proper court channels.

Although the DOD and its intelligence community have the same tools to trace back information warfare attacks as Law Enforcement; they must abide by US laws within the jurisdiction of the US. When an initial intrusion is identified, they are allowed to track back one connection to determine the immediate origination of the attack.[11] However, if the system is located within the US, the DOD is prohibited by US privacy laws to intrude into that system to determine the next link in the chain of attack. The following figure shows the geographic limitations, which restrict DOD in locating and identifying perpetrators of cyber attacks.

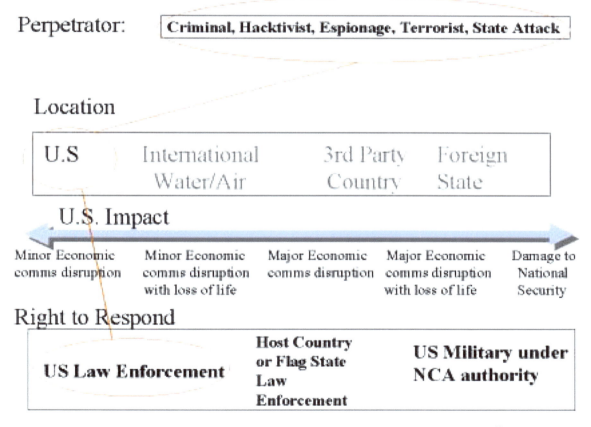

**Figure 3 Right to Respond if cyber attack occurs within US[12]**

The next figure shows that if the attack comes directly from overseas, DOD may trace and track the attack. However, if at any time the trace returns back to a US computer system, DOD must abide by US privacy laws[13].

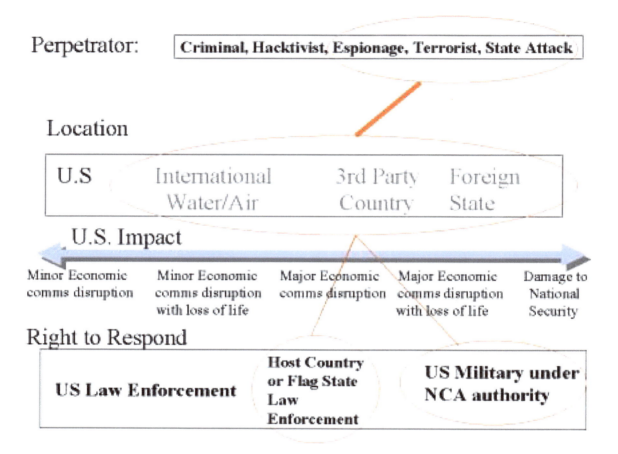

**Figure 4 Right to Respond if attack occurs from outside US[14]**

This distinction of US laws dictating the type of response for a computer attack against national and defense information structures is key to how the United States may defend and deter against cyber attacks. Geographic jurisdiction when locating and identifying the perpetrator is an important limitation when discussing the concept of defensive information warfare. Now the concept of computer attacks against the US has blurred the distinction between individual and state acts against the United States. In addition, a country may be at war with us in the sense of conducting information warfare attacks against our infrastructure and we may not know its identity. This is why it is

paramount that DOD build its own robust military criminal investigative organizations as

well as continue to work closely with the FBI to identify the perpetrator of cyber attacks.

Without this ability to identify and locate the perpetrator, it will be impossible for the US

to retaliate against cyber attackers.

## Notes

[1] Dorothy E. Denning and Peter F. Macdoran, "Grounding Cyberspace in the Physical World," in *Cyberwar: Security, Strategy, and Conflict in the Information Age,* ed. Alan D. Campen (Fairfax, VA: AFCEA International Press, 1998),119.

[2] Ibid.

[3] Ibid.

[4] Jim Christy, Supervisory Special Agent, Defense Wide Information Assurance Program, Assistant Secretary of Defense Command Control Communications and Intelligence (ASDC3I/DIAP), Pentagon interviewed by author, 14 November 2000.

[5] Denning, 184.

[6] "Carnivore Diagnostic Tool," FBI [Federal Bureau of Investigation] Report, n.p.; on-line, Internet, 17 January 2001, available from http: //www. fbi.gov/programs/ carnivore/carnivore2.htm

[7] Denning, 395.

[8] Ibid.

[9] Christy, interview by author.

[10] Ibid.

[11] Ibid.

[12] Ibid.

[13] Ibid.

[14] Ibid.

# Chapter 4

# Spectrum of Cyber Conflict

The purpose of developing a spectrum of cyber conflict is to show the range of cyber attacks from unintentional actors such as hackers and criminals with only self-serving interests to intentional actors with intent to affect national security. This spectrum will synthesize the type of attack, intentional or unintentional actors, location of attack, and will identify what agency will have the authority to identify and track down the perpetrator. It will also identify what type of appropriate response is likely to be taken by the US government against perpetrators ranging from criminal prosecution to extradition or a national policy response such as diplomatic, economic or military action against a state.

It is important to remember that any actor from a juvenile hacker to a sophisticated state intelligence service may have the capability to do extensive damage to our national information infrastructure and the capability to track and identify the perpetrator will always be extremely important regardless of the perpetrator's intentions. Sometimes, it may be as important to identify a criminal hacker with no national security interests as it may be to prove a state sponsored cyber warfare attack. Regardless, without the close coordination between DOD and law enforcement agencies, a quick and accurate response by the US government will not be possible.

Figure 5 depicts a spectrum of cyber conflict as discussed in this paper. The first discriminator is the type of attack. The type of attacks may range from cyber-crime to hacktivism, cyber-espionage, and cyber-terrorism all the way to cyber-warfare. The second distinction important to fully understand the cyber threat is the intention of the cyber actor (Unintentional vs. Intentional). Thirdly, it is paramount to identify the initial location of the attack and whether it is coming from within or outside the United States. These three factors (type of attack, intention of the perpetrator and location of perpetrator) will determine whether or not law enforcement or DOD initially responds to trace back the attack and will also affect the type of retaliation taken against the perpetrator. The following description will explain the Spectrum of Conflict as shown in Figure 5 below.

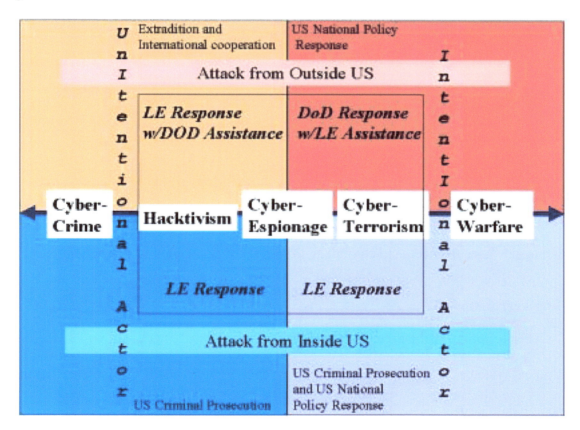

**Figure 5 Spectrum of Cyber Conflict**


25

# Type of Attack

## Cyber Crime

The first level of conflict is identified as Cyber crime and ranges from illegal exploration, hacking or other computer intrusions perpetrated by an individual or group with criminal or self-motivated interests and intent.

## Hacktivism

The second level of cyber conflict is a relatively new phenomenon identified as "hacktivism" and is politically motivated. Hacktivism is computerized activism and operates in the tradition of non-violent direct action and civil disobedience. It uses the same tactics of trespass and blockade from earlier social movements and applies them to the Internet. The aim of hacktivism is to draw attention to particular issues by engaging in actions that are unusual and will attract some degree of media coverage and possibly affect public or private actions. [1]

## Cyber-Espionage

Cyber-espionage is the use of computer hacking in foreign intelligence operations to obtain information or access to foreign computer systems with the intent to commit espionage or have the access to commit state sponsored sabotage when necessary.

## Cyber-Terrorism

Cyber-terrorism is the premeditated, politically motivated attack against information, computer systems, computer programs, and data, which result in violence against noncombatant targets by subnational groups or clandestine agents. [2]

**Cyber-Warfare**

Cyber warfare is defined as the "use of computer intrusion techniques and other capabilities against an adversary's information-based infrastructure"[3] to intentionally affect national security or to further operations against national security[4].

## Intention of Cyber-Actors

The intention of actors or perpetrators of cyber attack within the spectrum of cyber conflict can be broken down into two broad categories as relates to national security. These categories are outlined by Lionel D. Alford, Jr., in Appendix A of this paper and are defined as intentional cyber actors (I-actors) and unintentional cyber actors (U-actors).

> Intentional actors are individuals intentionally prosecuting attack through cyber-means to affect national security. U-actors are individuals who unintentionally attack but affect national security and are largely unaware of the international ramifications of their actions.[5]

Intention of perpetrators of a cyber attack is important as relates to the type of response by the US. Regardless of severe damage, if the perpetrator against a DOD system is determined to be a juvenile hacker from Great Britain who had no intention of causing damage to US national security, the US would not respond in-kind with a cyber-attack against the British Defense Establishment. However, if the Iraqi Intelligence Service in a cyber-warfare attack caused the same damage, the US may very likely consider an in-kind cyber attack or possibly a military retaliatory strike against Iraq. Obviously, it may be difficult to fully identity a perpetrator, especially if they are operating under the auspices of a foreign intelligence service, but if an attack could be traced back to a country such as Iraq, the US government could use this information for diplomatic, economic or military action. In most cases, an attack from an I-actor will be perpetrated through US computer systems and it will be paramount that US law enforcement agencies be involved in obtaining required court orders to trace back and establish the location and identity of the cyber attacker.

## Location of the Perpetrator (Outside or Within US)

As shown in figures 3 and 4, if the initial computer intrusion is identified as coming from outside the United States, the DOD does not violate any US laws by tracing the computer attack back to its source. However, if at any point during the trace back, the intrusion uses a computer system located within the US, DOD officials are not authorized by US law under the Privacy Act to obtain information from that system. At this point, appropriate law enforcement agencies would have to acquire court orders to obtain further information leading to the identification of the perpetrator.[6]

## Law Enforcement Response

The only case as shown in the Spectrum of Cyber Conflict diagram in which the DOD would initially respond to a cyber attack would be in the case of a serious attack coming from outside the United States. However, even in these circumstances, DOD officials must work closely with Law Enforcement in case the trace is eventually looped back to the United States. In addition, in most cases if the attack is determined to be located within an allied or friendly foreign country, a US law Enforcement agency such as the FBI or DOD investigative agencies will work with the law enforcement officials from that country to further locate and prosecute the attacker.

So as depicted in figure 5, US law enforcement officials in concert with DOD will be intricately involved in most cyber attacks against the national information infrastructure and DOD systems. This type of relationship between DOD and law enforcement must fundamentally change the understanding and nature of national security defense. It must also shape the way DOD prepares to defend and deter against information warfare attacks.

## Appropriate US Response

Finally, the spectrum of cyber conflict as depicted in figure 5 speaks to the type of appropriate response from the US government in case of a cyber attack. In most cases, the appropriate response will be prosecution of the perpetrator either within the United States or by extradition to the US or through appropriate courts in other countries. However, there will be times that the identity of the perpetrator reveals intent by a foreign government to do harm to US national security interests. It may then be appropriate for the US government to apply diplomatic or economic pressure towards the offending country or in certain circumstances retaliate in kind with a cyber attack or through military strikes.

The spectrum of cyber conflict as depicted above attempts to bridge the gap between computer attacks perpetrated with criminal intent and attacks with national security intentions. Both types of attacks are on the same spectrum of conflict and often are difficult to distinguish. Because of this continuum of conflict from crime to warfare, the US and its Department of Defense must be prepared to work within the full constraints of US law and still be able to respond and retaliate against would-be attackers. Without this capability, we will not be able to prevent and deter future attack.

## Notes

[1] Wray, n.p.
[2] Denning, 69.
[3] West, 17-18.
[4] Alford, 105.
[5] Ibid.
[6] Christy interview by author.

# Chapter 5

# Conclusion

*The state must make such disposition of its defense as will put it in the best possible condition to sustain any future war. But...these dispositions for defense must provide means of warfare suited to the character and form future wars may assume.*

—Giulio Douhet

To defend against all forms of cyber attack, the United States must have the ability to deter attacks. In most cases the first line of deterrence will be a strong defense to deny potential cyber attackers access to our systems. However, because of the inherently open nature of our systems, it will be impossible to stop all intrusions. As long as there is any risk for computer attack, we remain vulnerable. The second part of a strong deterrent policy will be the threat of retaliation or punishment. This ability to retaliate will be instrumental in establishing law and order in cyber space and will give us the ability to hold individuals, sub-state groups and states responsible for cyber attacks. Without this ability to retaliate, potential cyber attackers will continue to threaten US interests with impunity.

There are several technical and legal difficulties with identifying the perpetrator of a cyber attack. Because these attacks against our national information infrastructure and DOD networks are mainly perpetrated via computer intrusions from the Internet, it is very easy for the attacker to hide his identity through the World Wide Web. In addition, an attacker may also be able to hide his intentions by appearing to be a juvenile hacker but is actually collecting foreign intelligence or preparing for cyber warfare operations on behalf of a foreign government. Because of the difficulty in determining the type of attack without identifying the perpetrator, it is paramount to trace back the attack to the attacker.

Inherent in US law is the right to privacy, even on the Internet. The DOD is limited by US laws from obtaining information from computer systems located in the United States without proper legal authority, which can only be obtained via appropriate law enforcement agencies and US courts. Because of these legal restrictions, DOD must work closely with it's own investigative agencies and Department of Justice to be able to identify perpetrators and deter future attacks through the threat of punishment or military retaliation.

The spectrum of cyber conflict depicts the range of possible cyber attacks and identifies whether law enforcement or the military could pursue the attacker based on location of the attacker. It also shows the range of possible punishment or retaliation by DOD or the US government based on the perpetrator and his intentions to harm national security. The spectrum progresses from hackers with no intent to affect national security and advances to intentional actors like political activists who use hacktivism to affect changes in national policy. It then increases in threat to cyber espionage and cyber terrorism, which harms national security. Finally, it culminates with full out cyber warfare that furthers military operations (warfare) against a nation. The purpose of this spectrum is not only to depict the different types of computer attack but also to highlight the similarities between computer intrusions and reveal the need to identify not only the perpetrator but understand his intentions. This may not always be possible but in order to strengthen our deterrence of cyber attack, we must improve our ability to trace and identify attackers and retaliate through either criminal prosecution or other means of government sponsored retaliation when necessary.

# Appendix A

## A New Taxonomy of Cyber Terms

1. **Cyber warfare (CyW).** Any act intended to compel an opponent to fulfill our national will, executed against the software controlling processes within an opponent's system. CyW includes the following modes of cyber attack: cyber infiltration, cyber manipulation, cyber assault, and cyber raid.
2. **Cyber infiltration (CyL).** Penetration of the defenses of a software-controlled system such that the system can be manipulated, assaulted, or raided.
3. **Cyber manipulation (CyM).** Following infiltration, the control of a system via its software, which leaves the system intact, then uses the capabilities of the system to do damage. For example, using an electric utility's software to turn off power.
4. **Cyber assault (CyA).** Following infiltration, the destruction of software and data in the system, or attack on a system that damages the system capabilities. Includes viruses and overload of systems through email (email overflow).
5. **Cyber raid (CyR).** Following infiltration, the manipulation or acquisition of data within the system, which leaves the system intact, results in transfer, destruction, or alteration of data. For example, stealing email or taking password lists from a mail server.
6. **Cyber attack.** See CyL, CyM, CyA, or CyR.
7. **Cyber crime (CyC).** Cyber attacks without the intent to affect national security or to further operations against national security.
8. **Intentional cyber warfare attack (IA).** Any attack through cyber-means to intentionally affect national security (cyber warfare) or to further operations against national security. Includes cyber attacks by unintentional actors prompted by intentional actors. (Also see, "unintentional cyber warfare attack.")

   IA can be equated to warfare; it is national policy at the level of warfare. Unintentional attack is basically crime. UA may be committed by a bungling hacker or professional cyber criminal, but the intent is self-serving and not to further any specific national objective. This does not mean unintentional attacks cannot affect policy or have devastating effects.

9. **Intentional cyber actors (I-actors).** Individuals intentionally prosecuting cyber warfare (cyber operators, cyber troops, cyber warriors, cyber forces).
10. **Unintentional cyber actors (U-actors).** Individuals who unintentionally attack but affect national security and are largely unaware of the international ramifications of their actions. Unintentional actors may be influenced by I-actors

but are unaware they are being manipulated to participate in cyber operations. U-actors include anyone who commits CyL, CyM, CyA, and CyR without intent to affect national security or to further operations against national security. This group also includes individuals involved in CyC, journalists, and industrial spies. The threat of journalists and industrial spies against systems including unintentional attacks caused by their CyL efforts should be considered high.

11. **Unintentional cyber warfare attack (UA).** Any attack through cyber-means, without the intent to affect national security (cyber crime).[1]

## Notes

[1] Lt Col Lionel D. Alford, Jr., USAF, *Cyber Warfare: Protecting Military Systems,* **The Journal of the Defense Acquisition University,** Spring 2000, Review Quarterly, Vol 7, No. 2., page, 105

# Bibliography

Alford Lionel D., Jr., Lt. Col., USAF. "Cyber Warfare: Protecting Military Systems". *The Journal of the Defense Acquisition University Review Quarterly* 7. no. 2. Spring 2000.

Anderson, Robert H. et al. *Securing the U.S. Defense Information Infrastructure: A Proposed Approach.* Santa Monica, CA,: RAND, 1999.

Arquilla John, Ronfeldt David, and Zanini Michele. "Information Age Terrorism," in *Countering the New Terrorism.* Edited by. Ian O. Lesser et al. RAND Report MR-989-AF. Santa Monica, California: RAND, 1998.

Arquilla John. "Screen Saver." *New Republic*, 01 May 2000. Vol. 222. Issue 18. 1c. On-line. Academic Search Elite, 25 October 2000.

Bass, Carla D. Col., USAF. "Building Castles on Sand". *Airpower Journal* 13, no. 1 (Spring 1999): [27-45].

Barnett Roger W. "Information Operations, Deterrence, and the Use of Force". *Naval War College Review.* Spring 1998. n.p.; On-line. Internet. 13 November 2000. Available from http://www.nwc.navy.mil/press/review/1998/spring.

Campen, Alan d. and Dearth, Douglas H. ed. *Cyberwar 2.0: Myths, Mysteries and Reality.* Fairfax, VA,: AFCEA International Press, June 1998.

"Carnivore Diagnostic Tool." FBI [Federal Bureau of Investigation] Report, On-line. Internet, 17 January 2001. Available from http: //www. fbi.gov/programs/ carnivore/carnivore2.htm.

Coale, John C. "Fighting Cybercrime". *Military Review,* March – April 1998, 77.

"DARPA'S Emerald Proves Worth in Cyber Defense". *Washington (AFNP).* On-Line. Military Library FullTEXT, 25 October 2000.

Denning Dorothy E. *Information Warfare and Security.* Reading, MA.: Addison Wesley Longman, Inc., 1998.

Denning Dorothy E. and Macdoran Peter F. "Grounding Cyberspace in the Physical World". In *Cyberwar: Security, Strategy, and Conflict in the Information Age.* Edited by. Alan D. Campen. Fairfax, VA,: AFCEA International Press. 1998.

Grove, Gregory D., Goodman, Seymour E., and Lukasik, Stephen J. "Cyber-attacks and International Law." *Survival, The IISS Quarterly* 42, No. 3 (Autumn 2000)[89-108].

Glave, James "Anti-Nuke Cracker Strikes Again," *Wired News.* 3 July 98. On-line. Internet. 2 March 01. Available from http://www.thing.net/~rdom/ecd/Brithacker .html.

Kennedy, Kevin J., Lt Col, USAF, Lawlor, Bruce M., Col, USARNG, and Nelson, Arne J., Capt, USN. *Grand Strategy for Information Age National Security: Information Assurance for the Twenty-first Century.* Maxwell AFB, ALA,: Air University Press: August 1997.

Libicki Martin C. "Protecting the United States in Cyberspace". In *Cyberwar: Security, Strategy, and Conflict in the Information Age.* Edited by. Alan D. Capen, Douglas H. Dearth and R. Thomas Gooden. Fairfax, Virgina: AFCEA International Press, May 1996.

Libicki Martin C. *Defending Cyberspace and Other Metaphors.* The Center for Advanced Concepts and Technology. National Defense University. Washington D.C.: February 1997.

Parker Donn B. *Fighting Computer Crime.* New York: Wiley Computer Publishing, 1998.

President's Commission on Critical Infrastructure Protection. "Critical Foundations Protecting America's Infrastructures". On-line. Internet. 14 November 2000. Available on http: www.pccip.gov.

Rattray, Gregory J., Maj, USAF. "Strategic Information Warfare: Challenges for the United States". PhD diss., Air Force Institute of Technology, Wright Patterson AFB, OH, May 1998.

Shulman, Mark Russel. *Legal Constraints on Information Warfare.* Center for Strategy and Technology. Occasional Paper Number. 7. Maxwell AFB, Alabama: Air War College, March 1999.

West Robert C. "The cyber-defence force's virtual shield". *Janes Intelligence Review.* 01 December 2000. On-line. 2000 Jane's Information Group. 28 December 2000.

Wray Stephan. "Electronic Civil Disobedience and the World Wide Web of Hacktivism: A Mapping of Extraparliamentarian Direct Action Net Politics". *A paper for The world Wide Web and Contemporary Cultural Theory Conference.* Drake University: November 1998. On-line. Internet. 17 January 2001. Available from http: //www.nyu.edu/ projects/wray/ ecd.html.

www.ingramcontent.com/pod-product-compliance
Lightning Source LLC
Chambersburg PA
CBHW041424050326
40689CB00002B/641